Grace (God's definition)

Dedication

I want to always give all my praise and worship to my Lord and Savior Jesus Christ. Never would have made it this far without you Lord. I Love you with all my heart.

To my Mother who passed away recently: Mom, what more can I say but I miss you so much every day, and I pray that I can learn from your example of faithfulness to the Lord, to your community and to your family.

To my two brothers, and sister: We've all taken different paths in life, but one thing will never change: I love you all so much.

To Stacey, Victoria and Kayla: My three beautiful daughters: How I thank God and pray every day for you to be the best in everything you do. Never, ever give up on yourself.

To my Pastor and Breakthrough family: Thank you for making me feel at home. God, Bless you.

Chapter I

Amazing Grace, one of the most well-known church medley that has been sung in many different variations by so many recognized singers.

We used this word when we're sitting at the dinner table.

But what is Grace? And how important is it for us to understand the aspect of this word.

The Word of God declares that grace is much more than God's unmerited favor.

God's grace is the gift, the power, the anointing, and the equipment needed for ministry.

The word "Grace" comes from the Greek word "Charis", which means gratitude, benefit, favor, or gift given.

"Charis is derived from the Greek word "Charisma", which means a spiritual endowment or spiritual gift.

As believers in the Lord, we must be aware that our loving Heavenly Father has graced us with so much we can't thank Him enough.

We're going to focus on the different meaning of this word, as we go forth in His power to fulfil all that has been spoken over us in His precious Word.

Chapter II

Grace: Spiritual Blessing

1 Corinthians 1:3 (Kings James Version).

"Grace, and peace to you from God our Father, and the Lord Jesus Christ".

2 Corinthians 1:2 (Kings James Version).

"Grace and peace to you from God our Father, and the Lord Jesus Christ".

Galatians 1:3 (Kings James Version).

"Grace and peace to you from God our Father, and the Lord Jesus Christ".

Philippians 1:2 (Kings James Version).

"Grace and peace to you from God our Father, and the Lord Jesus Christ".

In the above-mentioned scriptures, the Apostle Paul begins with the salutation "Grace and peace be unto thee", grace defined in these scriptures are words or pronouncements of spiritual blessings upon the saints who were reading Paul's letters.

This is a very important lesson for all of God's people: Paul the Apostle, the most persecuted apostle in the Bible was pronouncing blessings on others while he himself was being beaten and whipped for the cause of Christ.

Salutation or pronouncement of spiritual blessing over our lives is very important, because circumstances will try to speak words of defeat to our hearts, but as we continue to speak blessings over our lives we will continue to stand on God's word of provision.

Ephesians 5:19 (Kings James Version).

"Speak to one another, in psalms, hymns and spiritual songs. Singing and make music to our hearts to the Lord, always giving thanks to God the Father for everything, in the name of our Lord Jesus Christ".

This scripture speaks on our everyday conversation. We who represents the Lord Jesus Christ must always be a source of encouragement to ourselves and each other. Psalms, hymns, and spiritual songs are used to edify, or make one rise like an edifice higher and higher.

The events that took place in the Old Testament concerning David, the man after God's own heart further solidify this important principle.

1 Samuel 30: 1, 2,6 (Kings James Version).

"Three days later, when David and his men arrived home at their town of Ziklag, they found that the Amalekites had made a raid into Negvev and Ziklag; they had crushed Ziklag and burned it into the ground. They had carried off the women and

children and everyone else but without killing anyone". (vs 6) "David was now in great danger because all his men were very bitter about losing their sons and daughters, and they began to talk of stoning him. But David encouraged himself in the Lord".

In this incident, King David had his entire family, and possessions stolen from him by his enemies, the soldiers that were with him were discouraged and angry. They turned their anger towards David, and wanted to stone him to death.

Imagine, going to work every day with people whose hearts are disappointed because life has not treated them right, or family members who are dealing with sickness, or other issues.

They don't need a sermon on tithing and offering, or five hundred ways to become a millionaire. What is needful to hear a word about a God who can turn around any tragedy into a triumph.

But before we can do that, we ourselves need to remember what the Lord has done for us.

That is what David did, he encouraged himself in the Lord, he distanced himself from all the negativity around him, and got alone with the same God who delivered him from the lion, the bear, and the giant Goliath.

The lesson we must gained from this example: Words matter. Prisons are filled with men and women who allowed words of disrespect cause them to commit crimes that brought them to the place where they are now. I've seen hundreds upon hundreds of videos of people attacking each other based on the words of another on social media outlets.

Proverbs 18:21 tells us "Death and life are in the power of the tongue, and they that love it shall eat the fruit of it".

David, the man after God's own heart shows us that no matter the storm or circumstance, we must always pronounce spiritual blessing upon ourselves.

When we do this on a consistent basis, we keep our focus on the God of our salvation, who has promised to never leave nor forsake us.

This will empower us to share what the Lord has done for us, encouraging them to know that He's more than able to do the same for them.

Chapter III

Grace: God's Insurance Policy

2 Corinthians 12:9 (Amplified Bible Version).

"But (The Lord) He has said to me, "My grace is sufficient for you [My lovingkindness and My mercy are more than enough--always available--regardless of the situation]; for [My] power is being perfected [and is completed and shows itself most effectively] in [your] weakness." Therefore, I will more gladly boast in my weaknesses, so that the power of Christ [may completely enfold me and] may dwell in me".

When we are first born (spiritually) we all received a birth certificate which stated the name of the person that gave birth to us, and it proves who we are and to whom we belong. Now at the time of our birth a policy was attached to our birth certificate and there was a reason why a policy was attached to a baby's birth certificate.

As we grew older, we found that we had a policy attached to the birth certificate. We did not know why it was attached and neither did we know how much it was for or what kind of policy it was.

Soon, we were old enough to go into the army, and there we needed special training, garments and equipment's for the tasks that we were assigned to.

When we received our garments, it consisted of: A **Breastplate**, which meant righteousness; a **Helmet** which meant salvation; a **Sword** which meant a divine word from our Chief Sergeant; a **Shield** which meant faith; **Gospel Shoes**; which meant or represented the Good News of peace where ever we go; a **Loin belt** which meant the written word that we received, which represented the Truth **(Scripture reference: Ephesians 6:13-17).** Our equipment was the endowment of the Holy Spirit (Scripture reference: Acts 1: 1-2,4), our helper, comforter, strength, and guide. After receiving our training, we were dressed and equipped for our task which was ahead of us. There was a slight problem: Our garments were not properly worn, so while we were out on the battlefield we took so many hits we were just about to give up. But we reached inside out garments and pulled out our birth certificate that had a policy attached to it, and across the middle in a small section it stated what type of policy was attached: **"Sufficient Grace Policy".** This policy let us know that we have a gift, an anointing, the power and equipment needed to complete our assignment. What we have, which was God's grace, was more than enough. It was **Sufficient!** So regardless of what kind of situation or battle we may be in or evidently face-God's Grace is Sufficient!!

God's grace helps us to wear our garment properly because He has graced all of us with different gifts.

(1) To one is given the power to speak a message of wisdom.

(2) To one is given the power to express a word of knowledge and understanding.

(3) To another the working of faith.

(4) To another extra ordinary power of healing.

(5) To another the workings of miracle.

(6) To another prophetic insight (The gift of interpreting the divine will and purpose).

(7) To another the ability to discern and distinguish between (the utterances of true) spirit (and false ones).

(8) To another various kind of (unknown tongues).

(9) To another the ability to interpret (such) tongues.

(Scripture reference: 1 Corinthians 12:11, Amplified Bible Version). So, we must be careful with the equipment that God has given us, and we must be careful how we use it also; for the equipment of God is very powerful. So, if we understand that God has graced (equipped) us for our ministry task, whatever comes our way **God's GRACE Is Sufficient!!!**

Chapter IV

Grace: Strength for the Journey

2 Peter 3:18 (Amplified Bible Version).

"But grow in grace (undeserved favor, spiritual strength) and recognition and knowledge and understanding of our Lord and Savior Jesus Christ (the Messiah). To Him (be) glory (honor, majesty, and splendor both here and now and to the day of eternity).

This walk with the Lord is an exciting adventure. Our relationship with the Lord should not be a boring, worn out unexciting trip, it should be as the Bible declares in **2 Corinthians 9:18**, a continual growth from faith to faith, and glory to glory.

The word "momentum" is defined as a continual, consistent, diligent progress towards one's goal and that should be the goal for all of God's children who are determined to reach their destiny in God.

The word "grace" is usually used to describe the unmerited favor of God, but the Apostle Peter also defined grace as spiritual strength.

This strength comes from the recognition and knowledge of our Lord and Savior Jesus Christ.

Divine momentum is the key to gaining spiritual strength. We must grow every day in the knowledge of our Lord and Savior Jesus Christ and the more we grow in our knowledge of who Jesus is, the more we can better appropriate His promises.

Growing in grace our spiritual strength will enable us to know that through Jesus Christ we are more than conquerors over every situation, and most importantly we will know that God is on our side!!

Our Christian growth should be like to riding an elevator, only stopping to pick up more revelation, wisdom, and understanding and dropping off any works of the flesh.

Grow in your walk with in Christ, make every day the best and most exciting day in your life as you gain spiritual strength and be what God has ordained you to be.

Chapter V

In the Biblical Dictionary, the number five is the number for Grace.

So, what does the Word **<u>"Grace"</u>** stands for:

 (1) <u>G</u>-Give God the Glory-No matter what the situation is, never lose your Praise!!

(2) <u>R</u>-Reap mercy and Joy-What you sow in others (love, forgiveness) you will reap a reward.

(3) <u>A</u>bound in every good work-God's grace enable us to complete the work He's called us to.

(4) <u>C</u>ount all things Joy-Find the blessing contained in every problem.

(5) <u>E</u>ndure all things-God's grace helps us to go through every trial and tribulation and always come out as winners!!

PRAYER

"Father, I thank you for the opportunity to share these truths with your children. Thank you for this gift of writing books to glorify your name and bless your people".

"I pray for the one reading, that they will continue to press on despite the circumstances, and valley they may be walking through".

"I pray you reveal yourself to them in a miraculous way, that you would open doors for them to bless your people".

"I speak your favor, blessing and increase be upon them continually in the name of Jesus Amen!!

Salvation Prayer

Perhaps you're reading this book, and you don't know Jesus Christ as your personal Lord and Savior.

You can. Jesus stands at the door, and He's knocking, let Him into your heart today.

Pray this simple prayer with me:

"Lord Jesus, come into my heart, be my Lord, my healer, my deliverer. Forgive me of my sins".

"I confess Jesus Christ as my Lord and Savior, and I believe God has raised Jesus up from dead, and He did it just for me".

"And per your word, I'm saved, I'm forgiven. I am a child of God. Thank you Lord for saving me today. I am saved".
If you prayed that pray for the first time, please send us an email, so we can rejoice with you.

I encourage you to find a church where the Word of God is being preached, so you can grow in your new walk with the Lord!!!

Welcome to the family.

LESSONS FROM
THE STORM
Mark Dudley

There is a blessing contained in every problem.
Find the seven blessings and learn there is victory
on the other side of through.

Dreams are for those who are willing to get out of their comfort zone and just "GO FOR IT".

Though you've been labeled by people, God has great plans for you.

These and all my books can be purchase on at inspired-word-ministry.com.